Table of Contents

Beautiful one,

Welcome to the next 21 days of stepping into your UNLEASHED. My prayer for you as you dig into this devotional is that you would begin to see yourself the way God sees you, as one that is enough, equipped, prepared, and not just adequate but more than adequate for what He has created and called you to. I pray that all striving will cease and that you will embrace WHOM God says you are and BE. I pray that your eyes will be opened to the greatest lie of all time – the lie that you have to fight and strive for something missing when God has already given you ALL you need. Nothing is lacking in you, daughter! I pray you see!

I love you so much and pray that you are free, healed, and whole through this devotional.

As you go through this devotional, I encourage you to create and speak these chapters over your life as prophetic declarations and affirmations until they sink into the core of your being and you begin to believe and operate from that space. You are who God says you are!

Walk in it, sis!

Your sister, in this journey,

Dr. MKW

I AM A PRICELESS
DAUGHTER OF THE
KING. I AM ONE OF A
KIND, A RARITY.

CHAPTER 1: PRICELESS

"WHO COULD EVER FIND A WIFE
(WOMAN) LIKE THIS ONE- SHE IS A
WOMAN OF STRENGTH AND MIGHTY
VALOR! SHE'S FULL OF WEALTH AND
WISDOM. THE PRICE PAID FOR HER
WAS GREATER THAN MANY
JEWELS."

PROVERBS 31:10 TPT

Chapter 1: Priceless

"A good woman is hard to find, and worth far more than diamonds." (Prov. 31:10 MSG)

What would happen if we would start seeing ourselves as our Maker sees us? What would happen if we saw ourselves as priceless and stopped aspiring to be worthy and valuable? Instead, we started to receive "priceless" as truth and as our identity as daughters of the Most High and carriers of His glory and DNA.

Let's take a look at what it means to be priceless. Sis, you are a good woman. A woman of strength and valor, full of wealth and wisdom, an excellent woman (one who is spiritual, capable, intelligent, and virtuous). A woman of noble character, a rarity, hard to find, competent, honorable, precious, paid for, and of great value.

Not because of anything you did but simply because you are a daughter of the King. He compares you to rubies, diamonds, precious stones, and pearls!

What would happen if you started seeing yourself as a valuable treasure in the sight of God? What would happen if you saw yourself as strong and full of virtue? What would happen if you recognized that within you lies wealth and wisdom and that you have been filled to the brim with this? You are not lacking in any way, daughter!!! What would happen if your eyes were opened to the fact that Christ paid a price for you worth so much more than all the jewels in this world? He gave His life for you because you mean that much to Him!

Many times, we operate from a place of striving and aspiring to be and find ourselves needing more compared to the standard we set for ourselves on how we think we should be or what we should be doing. What would happen if we were to embrace what we already are? That all we have to do...is be. What would happen if we begin to operate from a place of already "being" who God says we are?

The Father says today:
Daughter, You are worth it! You are valuable! You are priceless!

Father, I pray for my sister reading this today that You would bring a deeper revelation of your truth into her soul and spirit to realize just how beautiful and precious she is to You! Help her see that she doesn't have to compare herself to others or try hard to be something she aspires to, but realize she already is because You say so!

Let the questions in the reading today marinate in your soul for a few minutes, and then write what the Lord shows you. No filter! Allow God to whisper His truths in your ear and allow Him to begin reshaping your perspective of yourself! Lord shows you. No filter! Allow God to whisper His truths in your ear, and let him start reshaping your perspective of yourself!

> "
> You are not lacking in any way, daughter! You are worthy! You are valuable! You are priceless!
> "

I AM TRUSTWORTHY & ENRICH THE LIVES OF OTHERS

CHAPTER 2: TRUSTWORTHY

"HER HUSBAND (FAMILY & FRIENDS) CAN
TRUST HER, AND SHE WILL GREATLY ENRICH
HIS (THEIR) LIFE."

PROVERBS 31:11 NLT

Chapter 2: Trustworthy

I've always viewed the Proverbs 31 woman as someone I could never be because she appears to have it all together, and can I tell you, I DO NOT have it all together at all! I know many feel like this passage only applies to the married or those thinking of marriage...but what about the single lady or the one who does not want to get married? God started changing my perspective on this...

What would happen if you saw yourself as one who could be trusted? What if you saw "trustworthy" as part of your core identity and began to operate from this? This is not something to "do," but it is who He says you "are." What if you were to see yourself as one others can confide in and know it won't get to the gossip chatline?

Let's look at what it means to be trustworthy. Sis, this means that you can be relied upon to be honest and truthful, that you can provide what is needed or right in the moment, that you are worthy of confidence, that you are dependable, reliable, faithful, steadfast, and honorable. This means that you, my sister, are not a cheat or fraud, that you are a person of integrity, that you can be trusted with secrets or anything else of importance, including your assignment, that you are worthy of belief, and that your word can be trusted – you do what you say you will do!

For many of us, our identity has been shaped by past experiences that continue to whisper lies in our ears, shaping our perspective of ourselves. Often those lies include "I can't be trusted," "Gossip," "Betrayer," "Backstabber," "Cheat," "I have nothing of value to add to others," "I am nothing," "Parasite," "I always destroy everything and everyone around me," "I am a bad influence," & so many more! Yes, you may have "done" all that and more, but that is NOT who you are!

You are who God says you are! And today, He is reminding you of who He sees when He looks at you!

What if you saw yourself as that woman who instead took those things entrusted, revealed, and exposed to her to the cross, surrendering them at the throne? What would happen if you saw yourself as one whose presence enriches the lives of those she encounters? That people are made rich just by being in your presence and not by what you do because adding value to people's lives is in your DNA – it's simply who you are? You don't even have to try!!! You just have to BE!

Heavenly Father, I pray for my sister reading this today that You would reveal to her the identity that You, her Maker, bestow on her as one who can be trusted and whose life enriches the lives of all who encounter her! Wash away the residue of her past and confront the lies of the enemy that seek to keep her bound in what You have already paid for and covered in Your blood! Open her eyes to see herself as You see her!

Take a few moments today to sit and ask God to show you this and ask Him to rewire and reshape your perspective of yourself from what it has been for so long to who He declares you to be today – trustworthy and one who enriches others' lives! Write down how receiving and walking in these truths will change your life!

> "You may have done all that and more, but that is not who you are. You are who God says you are. You are altogether trustworthy, daughter."

I AM A COMFORT & ENCOURAGEMENT TO ALL I ENCOUNTER

CHAPTER 3: COMFORTER

"SHE COMFORTS, ENCOURAGES, AND
DOES HIM (THEM) ONLY GOOD AND
NOT EVIL ALL THE DAYS OF HER LIFE."

PROVERBS 31:12 AMP

Chapter 3: Comforter

How do you comfort, encourage, and do good, not harm to others ALL the days of your life when no one has done that for you? How do you do that when what you really hope for is that someone will do that for you? And you have no idea what being comforted, encouraged, and goodness feels or looks like? How do you do that when all you REALLY want to do is hurt those who hurt you, when the words running through your mind are those of pain-filled rage and curses towards those who have hurt and violated you, when everywhere you look, all you see are reminders of the bad done to you? This sometimes feels like too high of an expectation, and at times, your response to God may be, "Lord, why should I?"

Here's the good news... it's possible! How? When you look to your Maker as the source of all you need, including comfort, encouragement, and goodness! You may be saying, "That's nice, Mirriam, but I want something I can touch and feel." Or "Mirriam, that sounds super-spiritual and airy-fairy. I've tried that, and well... it's just not enough. It's not the same!" And believe me, I feel you! So here's a secret...in my most broken and messed up moments, when I was at my weakest and felt I had nothing to offer anyone and still chose to pour into someone, I found myself being filled as well! It's weird, but God works that way...when we give of ourselves and water the seeds of others, breathing life into others, we find that we are nourished! Because we know we don't have it, we look to God for strength to help others, and it's like we become a channel through which God's power flows, and as He flows through us, we are comforted, encouraged and become recipients of His goodness!

So today, what would happen if you saw yourself as He sees you – as one who comforts, encourages, and does good ALL the days of her life? What would happen if you saw yourself as BEING this not because you have to try so hard to DO this but simply because His DNA is within you and He says you ARE! This is who He says you are! Yes, this may not be your track record till this moment...you may be known as one who lashes out and hurts others with the words coming out of your mouth, and you may have started to believe that you are, at your core, bad! But today, God is inviting you to start afresh and allow Him to show you that your past does not define you! He says...He created...therefore you are!

Daughter, you inspire others with hope, courage, and confidence because you have received this from Me. Daughter, you are empowered to support, incite, and help others move forward because of what I have done for you and who I am within you.

Holy Spirit, today I pray for my sister that You would pour of Yourself into the deepest, broken places of her heart and help her to open up her heart and soul to You to be a vessel through which You comfort, encourage, and do good to those in desperate need. Lord, I ask that You would clean the slate today of all that the enemy has spoken over my sister, telling her she has nothing to offer because she has never experienced this for herself. Please help her receive from You ALL that she needs in this moment. Surround her with Your love and heal those broken places, comforting her today and encouraging her spirit. May she see Your goodness going before her today, pursuing her! Open her eyes to Your goodness in her life, even amid hardship and pain! Let Your love pierce through, and let Your light shine brightly in and through Your daughter today!

Take some time today to sit with God regarding this.
Journal about what He shows you! Share below what
He reveals to you to encourage and comfort someone
else today...and you are well on your way to walking in
your identity as a comforter, encourager, and one who
does good!

> God is inviting you to start
> afresh and allow Him to show
> you that your past does not
> define you! He says...He
> created...therefore you are!

I AM SKILLED IN WHAT
I HAVE BEEN ASSIGNED
TO DO &
DEMONSTRATE
EXCELLENCE IN
WHATEVER MY HANDS
FIND TO DO

CHAPTER 4: SKILLED

"SHE SEARCHES OUT CONTINUALLY
TO POSSESS THAT WHICH IS PURE
AND RIGHTEOUS. SHE DELIGHTS IN THE
WORK OF HER HANDS."

PROVERBS 31:13 TPT

Chapter 4: Skilled

What does wool and flax have to do with anything, right? And what is flax anyway? In Bible days, wool was used to create outer garments and flax for inner garments, and learning this skill of spinning and creating material and garments was a critical skill every young woman needed to learn to clothe her household. Not everyone excelled at this, but those who did were able to create profitable businesses that could not just clothe her family but sustain them and prosper them to be a blessing to others. In today's world, this skill may be considered unnecessary or minute, but without it, none of us would have the clothes we wear. Most of us don't even think twice about how our clothes are created, especially the fabric itself, as long as it's a designer label. But somewhere, someone picked the wool and flax and spun it into the thread that became fabric.

Like some or many of you, my mom made sure I learned how to sew, knit, and crochet when I was a teen, but please do not ask me to do it today because I could not tell you how! It's been a minute since I picked up any needles. Still, God showed me that this does not necessarily mean steel needles...this Scripture refers to seeking and finding with all your heart, mind, soul, and body that skill and that thing you were created to do – in its pureness and God-intended way – and when you find it doing it will all that you have within you to the best of your God-given ability. "What you are is God's gift to you, and what you become is your gift to God." (Hans Urs von Balthasar)

What does being skilled mean? Sis, it means that you have what it takes in knowledge, ability, and training to do something well because God has equipped you for this very moment you are in. It means that God delights in your diligent efforts and has blessed the work of your hands so that you may be a blessing. You can have joy in your work!!!

What would happen if you were to believe that there is a skill that God gave you, a skill you can learn, a skill that will not only put food on your table but also clothe others and overflow blessings into areas and regions you won't even fully comprehend in your lifetime? What would happen if you were to believe that all it takes is one step at a time, one day at a time, one moment at a time, picking up your "needles," harnessing and perfecting that skill, and then working that skill diligently to the fulness of your ability to not only change your life but the lives of others around you? What if you were to believe that God's narrative about you says, "You are equipped," "You are not lazy," "You are not useless," "You are not worthless," and "You are well able!" It's in your DNA, daughter of the Most High!

It may start with just creating one thing and then another, putting one foot in front of another, using what is in your hand! It may be cleaning, cooking, baking, singing, writing, talking, or gardening...it may be even knitting, crocheting, or sewing! It may be organizing! Start where you are with what you have. Do one thing and do it well! Now, do it in service to others and do it with diligence and excellence! Allow God to turn that one thing into what puts bread on your table and brings blessings to others! Teach someone what you have learned! Now, teach another and another. It just takes one! One thing done exceptionally well with all your effort! GET EXCITED ABOUT IT! Delight in it!!!

Father, help my sister see what You have placed in her hands to do and find her one – the place to start creating something from what You have already placed in her hands to do! May she work it and work it diligently. May she demonstrate hard work and perseverance because You engraved that nature in her when You created her in Your likeness! She is skilled and equipped to be all You created her to be!

Take some time with God today, asking Him to show you what He has skilled you with. Ask Him to show you how to start with one and how to serve the world with your one. Write this below.

Now that you know...go do it!
Journal your experiences daily!
Document your journey because one day, your testimony will bless others and bring freedom to others who feel stuck just like you today!

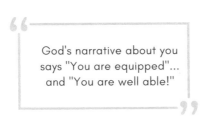

God's narrative about you says "You are equipped"... and "You are well able!"

I AM FILLED WITH THE
SPIRIT OF WISDOM &
AM RESOURCEFUL,
CAPABLE OF DEVISING
INNOVATIVE
STRATEGIES TO
RESOLVE DIFFICULT
SITUATIONS

CHAPTER 5: RESOURCEFUL

"SHE GIVES OUT REVELATION-TRUTH
TO FEED OTHERS. SHE IS LIKE A
TRADING SHIP BRINGING DIVINE
SUPPLIES FROM THE MERCHANT."

PROVERBS 31:14 TPT

Chapter 5: Wise & Resourceful

Today, God says you are wise because you have the mind of Christ and because His Spirit lives within you! You are a student of the Word, studying to show yourself approved and able to discern right from wrong because you continually renew your mind with His truth by the revelation of His Holy Spirit that dwells within you! His Spirit teaches and instructs you, showing you which way to go.

You are resourceful, finding the best deals, and filled with creativity to know how to put things together, where to source supplies, and equipped to make your ideas and business concepts successful! You don't give up at the first sign of trouble but push through to find solutions. You do your research and put in the work, carefully weighing your options and seeking wise and Godly counsel before you make decisions! Because of this, none that surround you go hungry, but all that are connected to you are fed! They lack for nothing! Your success overflows to bless all those associated with you! This is who God sees when He looks at you!

Take a moment to receive this, read over the above several times until it saturates your mind and Spirit, and allow God to speak His truth to you! Replace the "you" with "I" and declare this over yourself several times until it sinks in!

It does not matter that before today, your decisions and moves may have all "failed" or that you felt stuck and lacking resources to do the things you wanted to do. What matters today is that you begin to see yourself as He sees you and know that you have His Spirit living and dwelling within you, and because of this, you have ALL you need to prosper and succeed in what you were created for! You have to see this and believe this!

Ask God to help you overcome all doubts and fears. Ask Him to open your ears to hear His voice instructing and leading you. Ask Him to open your eyes to see opportunities where others see a dead end and failure. Now sit, be still, and listen for His directive. He is always speaking, sometimes in the most unexpected way. We need to be willing to hear what He is saying.

Father, I pray for my sister today that You would pierce through every lie that has been spoken over her and every lie she has believed that causes her to doubt her sanity and resourcefulness. I silence the voices that constantly shout "failure," "stupid," or "lacking" and replace those with the truth that she has the mind of Christ and that she has all she needs to fulfill her assignment. I ask that You give her the courage to challenge her doubts and fears and that You open her eyes to see the opportunities and solutions You have placed before her. Open her ears to hear Your voice leading her in the path she should take, remove all distractions, and silence the noise. Thank You for her insight and innovativeness and for not making anything too difficult for her.

Write down what you hear god saying about the situation you are in right now. Write down the ideas He shows you and the answers/solutions/resources He reveals. Keep listening and write down His directions. Now follow them and write down what happens next. to you. Keep listening and write down His directions. Now, follow them and write down what happens next.

" What matters today is that you begin
to see yourself as He sees you and
know that you have His Spirit living
and dwelling within you and because
of this, you have ALL you need to
prosper and succeed in what you
were created for! "

I AM PREPARED BY
HOLY SPIRIT,
EQUIPPED &
POSITIONED WITH
PROVISION FOR
WHATEVER COMES MY
WAY. GOD IS MY
SOURCE.

CHAPTER 6: PREPARED

"EVEN IN THE NIGHT SEASON SHE
ARISES AND SETS FOOD ON THE
TABLE FOR HUNGRY ONES IN HER
HOUSE AND FOR OTHERS."

PROVERBS 31:15 TPT

Chapter 6: Prepared

"She's up before dawn, preparing breakfast for her family and organizing her day." (Proverbs 31:15 MSG)

What do you think about starting your day early? I will be the first to admit that even though I grew up waking up and starting my day early, lately, I have been slacking and hitting the snooze button, snuggling in for an extra 5 minutes, which turns into 30 minutes, and before I know it, I am rushing to get ready for work. And the rest of my day looks and feels the same – rushed, unprepared, frantic, and exhausting!

But... when I rise early and spend time with my Maker getting my instructions for the day and positioning myself to be filled before I pour out, I am energized, prepared, equipped, and ready for whatever the day throws at me! Even in (especially in) my darkest seasons, when I feel like I have nothing to give because I am going through it myself, when I start my day right and with a plan, especially His plan, I can set the table before those assigned to me! I can feed others when I have been fed myself. I can pour out rivers of living water when I have drunk from the stream of Living Waters and had my fill from the spring that will never run dry!

What about you? What is or isn't working in your routine and daily schedule today? Take some time to sit with God today and examine your day...Are you pouring from an empty cup? Are you trying to feed others from a place of starvation yourself? Are you just going with the flow without taking directives and assignments from your Maker for your day? How is it working out for you? If it's going great, awesome! If not, what may you adjust to begin commanding your days differently? I'm not saying everyone should wake up early...but what if you did?

Everyone has their moments of optimal productivity...what is yours? Several scriptures and even Jesus showed us the importance of starting our day right. A proverb says, "The early bird catches the worm." What might a slight adjustment to how you begin each day transform your life?

This is what the Father wants you to know: Daughter, I desire to prepare you for what lies ahead of you. Come sit with Me awhile! Let Me fill you and equip you for the assignment allocated to you. All you need is found in Me!

Holy Spirit, You are the spirit of revelation and truth. Please show my sister today the areas that need adjustment to help her be better prepared for her day so that she can maximize the opportunities You bring her way. Please help her begin and end with You and take authority over her day, trusting You for a day that aligns with Your plan for her life. Help her realize that she is not helpless nor a victim of her situation but that You have given her all power to change her life, one action at a time.

Take a moment to reflect on your preparation &
positioning for your day. What adjustments in your routine
and schedule may you need to make to position yourself
to serve the world better from a prepared place? What is
ONE action you can take today? Better from a prepared
place? What is ONE action you can take today?

"
When I start my day right and with
a plan, especially His plan, I am
able to set a table before those
assigned to me!
"

I AM A WISE, SPIRIT-LED INVESTOR. OUT OF THE ABUNDANCE & SURPLUS OF MY GOD-RESOURCES, I MAKE PROFITABLE INVESTMENTS THAT IMPACT GENERATIONS TO COME.

CHAPTER 7: INVESTOR

"SHE LOOKS OVER A FIELD AND BUYS
IT, THEN, WITH MONEY SHE'S PUT
ASIDE, PLANTS A GARDEN."

PROVERBS 31:16 MSG

Chapter 7: Investor

Daughter, you are a wise investor in your finances! You do not waste money or spend money frivolously! Instead, you SAVE and have the money to invest in property and business! You take the time to consider and weigh investment and business ventures, doing your research thoroughly and making informed decisions. You put money aside and plant gardens that feed you, your family, and those around you! You do not need to borrow money or get into debt doing this because you have learned the skill of saving and building one block at a time, using what is in your hands! You understand that you are building for generations to come, so you build that which will endure and last. You are not interested in get-rich-fast schemes!

""he sets her heart upon a nation and takes it as her own, carrying it within her. She labors there to plant the living vines.""
(Proverbs 31:16 TPT)

Because of your discipline and obedience regarding how you spend your money, your finances are blessed, and you lack for nothing! You see a need and cause and carry it in your spirit until it gives birth to purpose. You are a hard worker, purchasing seeds, tilling the soil, weeding the field, and watching and praying over the dreams God has deposited in your heart until it produces a harvest of life, love, joy, and peace! You are an intercessor! You know how to keep things God reveals in your heart until the right time! You aren't concerned about what people think and aren't trying to win them over! You have an assignment and mission, and that is your only priority! Whatever your hands find to do is blessed! You are victorious and prosperous in everything you set your mind to do! You are a daughter of the King, His chosen one! Yes, you!

I love how the Amplified Classic words this scripture: "She considers a [new] field before she buys or accepts it [expanding prudently and not courting neglect of her present duties by assuming other duties]; with her savings [of time and strength] she plants fruitful vines in her vineyard."

What comes to mind when you read the above? What would change in your approach to life if you were to believe this as the truth about who you are and who you were created to be? If you saw yourself through these lenses, that savings are not just monetary but also involve the time and strength you need to invest in cultivating life and fruit-bearing vines in your own life. This is not a waste of investment!

I understand that this may only be the narrative of your story up to this moment! Your story may be the opposite of every aspect above, and maybe you've even adopted this as your nature...assigning labels such as wasteful, lazy, unlucky in business, failure, going nowhere, etc., to yourself. But you can choose life today and decide that your story regarding finances will be different from this moment onwards.

Father, thank You for changing my sister's story with money and her resources of time and strength! Thank You for giving her the ability and will to make wise choices regarding her finances, time, and energy. I declare that she is blessed and that her bank account and energy tank are overflowing because she consults with You regarding her investments and engagements in various ventures. Thank You for giving her the ability to make sound and strategic investments that will build generational wealth and create room for her to be a blessing to many. Thank You for making my sister a good steward of everything You entrust her with. Thank You that she multiplies every seed she has and that You constantly give her ideas on creating wealth. She lacks for nothing!

Take some time today to sit with God regarding your finances and spending habits. Ask Him to show you the areas where you need to make some changes. Write these below and seek Him for specific actions you need to take to change your story one step at a time.

Now, take action and document your journey as you apply His direction and the results you see in your life!

> You have learnt the skill of saving and building one block at a time, using what is in your hands! You understand that you are building for generations to come, and so you build that which will endure and last.

I AM STRONG IN THE LORD & IN THE POWER OF HIS MIGHT. HIS JOY IS MY STRENGTH! I AM SPIRITUALLY, MENTALLY, EMOTIONALLY & PHYSICALLY FIT FOR MY GOD-GIVEN ASSIGNMENTS!

CHAPTER 8: STRONG & INDUSTRIOUS

"SHE EQUIPS HERSELF WITH STRENGTH
[SPIRITUAL, MENTAL, AND PHYSICAL
FITNESS FOR HER GOD-GIVEN TASK] AND
MAKES HER ARMS STRONG."

PROVERBS 31:17 AMP

Chapter 8: Strong & Industrious

Woman of God, daughter of Zion, you are fierce and strong! Like a lioness that rises to defend and fend for her tribe, the Spirit of the Most High rises within you as you sit in My presence (GOD), drawing from Me the strength you need for this day! You may feel weak and powerless, and the enemy may whisper lies to that effect in your ear because your strength and vigor terrifies him. It is in your most fragile and most vulnerable moments, daughter, that My strength is made perfect in you and revealed to you because it is in those moments when you come to the end of your wisdom and your ability that you look to Me and feel like you have to draw strength from Me. If only you would realize that I am always present, always with you, always your source, always seeking to empower and strengthen you for the battle before you!

I am your portion! I am your strength! I am your wisdom! I am your creativity! I am that I am, and I am your God! And because I am and I dwell within you, you are! You are well able! You lack nothing! Draw from Me and find in Me all that you desire and need! Strengthen yourself in My presence! Sit a moment with me and soak in My love for you! Be still, daughter, and know my strength! Know Me!

""he is energetic and strong, a hard worker."" (Proverbs 31:17 NLT)
""First thing in the morning she dresses for work, rolls up her sleeves, eager to get started."" (Proverbs 31:17 MSG)

Today, let this word saturate and infuse every part of your being! Allow God to breathe over every area of weakness and weariness! Put some worship music on, sit with God, and be still. Rest in this truth! He is with you! You are not alone. You do not have to fight alone. You don't have to struggle. Lean into His strength today!

"In conclusion, be strong in the Lord [draw your strength from Him and be empowered through your union with Him] and in the power of His [boundless] might." (Ephesians 6:10 AMP)

Holy Spirit, You are the Spirit of life that raised Jesus from the dead! Minister to the areas of weariness and dryness in my sister's life today. Breathe life into her soul and bones. In those areas where she feels like she cannot go on, I ask that You strengthen her and give her the grace to push through. Help her to draw strength from You and find rest in the pause of just sitting with You when chaos seems to be raging around her. Let her know that she is safe, for You are with her. Help her lean into You and receive the strength You long to pour into her today.

Find a quiet space and close your eyes. Allow Him to speak into your dry places and allow His presence to enfold and cover you! Take a deep breath in and let it out slowly. Take another one. And another and sit meditating on this Word. Listen. And then write what He is showing you and speaking to your soul.

> Daughter, you are equipped
> with strength in spirit, soul, and
> body to complete the the
> assignment I have set before
> you.

I AM A
UNEXTINGUISHABLE
RADIANT LIGHT,
CREATED TO RADIATE
THE GLORY OF GOD
THROUGH THE WORK
OF MY HANDS.
I AM UNSTOPPABLE.

CHAPTER 9: RADIANT & UNSTOPPABLE LIGHT

"SHE TASTES AND EXPERIENCES A BETTER
SUBSTANCE, AND HER SHINING LIGHT WILL
NOT BE EXTINGUISHED, NO MATTER HOW
DARK THE NIGHT."

PROVERBS 31:18 TPT

Chapter 9: Radiant & Unstoppable Light

Daughter, you are valuable, and that which you create and produce is of great value, for it comes from me. You are excellent and beautiful, and the work of your hands is blessed! Whatever your hands find to do, you do with zeal and excellence! You add value to all those that come into contact with you! You are constantly seeking to do good and not harm. You recognize that you were created as the answer and the solution to various situations – a heavenly response to an earthly problem.! You add value to all those who come into contact with you! You are constantly seeking to do good and not harm. You recognize that you were created as the answer and the solution to various situations – a heavenly response to an earthly problem.

You are aware and cognizant of the truth embedded within you, which is everything you need to be precisely that – the answer, the solution, the response. You are skilled and equipped from creation and conception with all you need to succeed in your assignment! This knowledge and revelation of who you are fuels and defines your daily schedule. You are inspired and full of energy and excitement because you realize that you are a blessing to many simply because you are you! You cannot wait to get up and face your day because you know you have something of value to contribute to the world!

"She sees that her gain is good; Her lamp does not go out, but it burns continually through the night [she is prepared for whatever lies ahead]." (Proverbs 31:18 AMP)

No matter how dark the night, your light does not go out! You shine brightly!!! Because living and breathing in and through you in the very Light of the World! You are simply the carrier of His glory! So, shine, daughter, and do not hold back or hide! You are valuable!

"She knows the value of everything she makes, and works late into the night." (Proverbs 31:18 GNB)

"She senses the worth of her work, and is in no hurry to call it quits for the day." (Proverbs 31:18 MSG)

There's just something about knowing the value you bring to the table and the fierceness that accompanies this revelation. You become unstoppable and relentless in your fight against darkness. No matter what comes against you or how dark the night, you press in and know that you cannot and will not be turned off, dampened, silenced, or stopped. Darkness can never out-power light! My sister, you are unextinguishable because of the Holy Spirit within you!

Read over the above paragraph over and over until it registers in your spirit. Read it out loud! Allow God to rewire your thinking! Allow Him to show you your worth! Allow Him to open your eyes to the treasure He has placed on the inside of you! You are valuable! How does this resonate within you?

Lord, open my sister's eyes so that she would see herself the way You see her. Let her recognize Your light within her, and may she have the courage to shine that light brightly! Show her that she is the answer someone has been praying for; she is not a mistake but Your divine creation, and that divine destiny is connected to her. Please give her a revelation of what she carries within her and the impact that her gift shall have on the world so that she is energized to get up each day with excitement about what may unfold as she encounters those You place in her on the world so that she is energized to get up each day with excitement to what may develop as she encounters those You place in her path.

Take some time today to write the following statement: "I am a radiant and unstoppable light!"

Read and write it repeatedly, allowing the Holy Spirit to speak to you. Listen to His voice. Yes, you hear Him speaking! Write down what He is saying to you! Read it over. Meditate on it and write down how this is changing your perspective and approach to life. your perspective and approach to life.

> Daughter, you are valuable and that which you create and produce is of great value for it comes from me.

I AM AN EFFICIENT
ADMINISTRATOR OF
THE GIFTS AND
RESOURCES
ENTRUSTED TO ME. I
DEMONSTRATE
EXCELLENCE IN
WHATEVER MY HANDS
FIND TO DO.

CHAPTER 10: EFFICIENT ADMINISTRATOR

"SHE SPINS HER OWN THREAD AND
WEAVES HER OWN CLOTH."

PROVERBS 31:19 GNB

Chapter 10: Efficient Administrator

This is a controversial one! So feel free to disagree. I need to learn about spinning, weaving, and home crafts. Homemaking, as traditionally defined, is totally not my thing, BUT when I read The Passion Translation, I was like, "YES! This I can do!"

"she stretches out her hands to help the needy, and she lays hold of the wheels of government." (Proverbs 31:19 TPT)

I am passionate about meeting the needs of those with more significant difficulties accessing the resources they need and influencing culture and policy at various levels. I absolutely love serving others and helping people heal and find purpose and meaning in life! I also love the arts, and serving in the house of God.

"She's skilled in the crafts of home and hearth, diligent in homemaking." (Proverbs 31:19 MSG)

Traditionally speaking, I often find myself lacking in what my mind perceives as the skilled homemaker, but I have come to embrace the fact that I do not have to be like anyone else. I can be me. I can be excellent and skilled in the areas God has gifted me. I do not like doing laundry, but I love cooking and doing dishes. I do not like ironing!!! And cleaning is not something I am passionate about, even though I cannot stand a messy house! No matter how much I try, I cannot be excited about dusting and mopping...even my back complains, lol!

But I do know what I love and what I am good at, and I do all I can to grow, develop, and serve excellently. I used to feel shame and guilt for even thinking about paying someone to clean my house, but now I weigh my options, and I am ok with it if it means I get to enjoy a clean house and spend quality time with my hubby. I DO NOT have to have it all together all the time, and I can ask for help when I need it...especially in areas of my weakness and intense dislike. It's ok to order a pizza now and then! I am not the traditional wife, and that is ok! But I am still a woman of great virtue and excellence, working with all my might at those things that God has specifically assigned to me in this season, and I can still make my home a haven of rest.

Father, help my sister embrace her weird, the good, the bad, and the ugly, including those areas that, for a long time, have brought shame and guilt because they did not match up to what she felt she should be able to do as a woman. Help Your daughter see that none of these determine her worth but that You have given her the ability to be resourceful in asking for help and support in the areas where she lacks skill. Thank You for the wisdom You give her to make her house into a haven in which she and her family can find rest. Let grace be extended to herself in this area and to those who may not be as capable as her. Help her administer the gifts and resources You entrusted her with excellent efficiency and wisdom.

What areas have you been beating yourself over because you were not all together in it? Which areas of traditional homemaking do you not particularly enjoy that you could ask for help in or delegate to others so you can focus your energy on whatyou are gifted in and excel in? What are your strengths...the things you love fiercely and are gifted and good at doing? How can you develop further in these areas? How will your excellence in these areas impact your world? Take a few minutes to note this down below.

> "
> I DO NOT have to have it all together all the time and I can ask for help when I need it...especially in areas of my weakness and strong dislike.
> "

I AM A GIVER & AM
BLESSED WITH AN
ABUNDANCE TO SOW
MEANINGFULLY INTO
THE LIVES OF OTHERS.

CHAPTER 11: GENEROUS

"SHE IS KNOWN BY HER
EXTRAVAGANT GENEROSITY TO THE
POOR, FOR SHE ALWAYS REACHES
OUT HER HANDS TO THOSE IN NEED."

PROVERBS 31:20 TPT

Chapter 11: Generous

Daughter, you are extravagantly generous!!! The desire to nurture and care for those around you is embedded within you. You constantly give of yourself, even from what seems like lack. When you see a need, you are prompted to action! Many times, you wish you could do more. Sometimes, you look at what is in your hand and feel inadequate, ill-equipped, and lacking resources. There are moments when you compare yourself to others and feel like what you have to offer is insignificant. But I want you to realize today that what you have is seed. And you never know the potential of seed by just looking at it.

"This generous God who supplies abundant seed for the farmer, which becomes bread for our meals, is even more extravagant toward you. First, He supplies every need, plus more. Then He multiplies the seed as you sow it, so that the harvest of your generosity will grow."
(2 Corinthians 9:10)

This is what the Father wants you to know: I have given you seed! You have been created with the ability to produce seed. You are lacking nothing for it is embedded within My design of you.

Stop underestimating and downplaying the power and potential of your seed. Stop allowing the lies of the enemy that minimize the value of your seed to prevent you from sowing the seed you have in the ground that is before you. A mustard seed is so small but brings forth a great tree. I have created you with the ability to take seed (what I have placed in your hands) and create life from it, giving birth to things the extent of its influence and impact you will never fully comprehend in your lifetime.

Stop comparing your seed to another's seed. It may look like just a cup of water, just a sandwich, just a hug, just a smile, just a text, just $10... but a little placed in the hands of an Almighty God is much! Just work your ground with what I have placed in your hands. Then watch Me work!!!

Father, I pray that You would open my sister's eyes to see the seed You have placed in her hands. Help her recognize that little in Your hands is much and that when she sows what she has in the areas that You are instructing her to deposit, she can trust that You will show her how to nurture and grow the seed into a harvest. Father, I pray You will show Your daughter that You are also sending others to water and nurture those seeds. Help Your daughter see that multiplication can only happen when she takes what You have given her and sows it, not underestimating the power of her seed. Show her that she has all she needs to make an impact. Show her that her generosity is not in the abundance of her seed but in her willingness to surrender her little to You.

What seed has God embedded within His design of you? Sit with God and ask God to reveal what He has already placed within you. What is God bringing to remembrance? In what ways is God challenging you to walk in generosity? Write this in your journal or in the space below.

> "Stop comparing your seed to another's seed...Just work your own ground with what I have placed in your hands. Then watch me work!!!"

I AM A FEARLESS
BECAUSE I AM
COVERED. I AM SAFE
AND PROTECTED BY
THE ALMIGHTY.
THE BLOOD OF JESUS &
HIS GRACE COVER ME
CONTINUOSLY.

CHAPTER 12: FEARLESS

"SHE IS NOT AFRAID OF TRIBULATION,
FOR ALL HER HOUSEHOLD IS COVERED
IN THE DUAL GARMENTS OF
RIGHTEOUSNESS AND GRACE."

PROVERBS 31:21 TPT

Chapter 12: Fearless

Bring it on!!! Come trials, tribulations, winter seasons, storms...whatever may... sister, dare to be fearless!

Daughter, there is no need to be afraid. Fear is not your portion. I have paid the price to ensure your protection as well as the protection of those connected to you! I have torn the veil granting you access to My presence. When you stay in alignment with Me, abiding under My shadow, no harm will come near you, and even if they try, they will not succeed! You have access to My blood, the symbol of My sacrifice and the price I paid for you, and at the mention of My name every knee must bow. When the enemy looks at you, he sees Me and will not harm you. No matter how fierce the battle and the chaos around you, remember My blood and My name speak louder than every other voice. When you stay under My covering and stay connected to Me, I go before you, fighting on your behalf.

Daughter, when you pray, standing in the gap covering others, angels are dispatched on your behalf! No matter where they may be, heaven responds on your behalf to protect those you love. When you pray for your loved ones, you are never afraid because you know I am watching over them, and they are covered. Train up your household! Teach them about Me. Introduce them to Me. When you know they know Me, you know that they have Me no matter where they are, and they are safe no matter what comes their way. When you know your family is covered in the blood, there is no need to fear! You overcome by the blood and the word of your testimony!

Sis... What would you do if you believed that you are fearless? Above all, what would happen if you got a revelation of what it means to walk under the shadow of God Almighty? What feats would you accomplish? What mountains would you climb, what doors would you push through, what dreams would you pursue?

Nothing can touch you or even try to come near you without the Father's approval! And know this: when it comes your way, it has already been vetted by the Father as something that will pull out of your something (strengths, gifts, anointing, etc.) He already knows what is within you because He built it in there, or that it will deliver for you something (opportunities, treasures, victories, etc) that He already knows you have been equipped to handle. He's already prepared a table and made a way! It's a done deal! Every tribulation is a God set up!

Father, break through the fear and doubt that seeks to cripple my sister. Set her free so that she may not be trapped by fear. Teach her to war in the spirit and to take her position under Your covering with authority and power. Reveal areas in her life that are out of alignment with You and show her how to bring everything You have entrusted to her under Your covering and trust You with all of it. Show her that her greatest weapon is her connection to You and that most battles are best fought in prayer, and show her how to wield her sword to tear down every lie of the enemy with Your truth. May she walk in boldness and complete confidence, knowing You have her back!

Are there areas of your life and family that continue to cause you fear and anxiety? Write these down. In what ways is God challenging you to shift your perspective on these trials? Are there those in your circle who do not know God? In what ways is your trial a setup for you to introduce someone to Jesus and make sure they are covered by the blood and properly aligned with His will? Journal these thoughts below or in your journal.

"Daughter, there is no need to be afraid. Fear is not your portion...I have you covered!"

I AM ROYALTY,
CREATED IN THE IMAGE
& LIKENESS OF GOD.
I SET THE TONE OF
EVERY ROOM I WALK
INTO WITH CREATIVITY
& INNOVATION. I AM
A TRENDSETTER &
WORLD CHANGER.

CHAPTER 13: CLASSY, INNOVATIVE TRENDSETTER

"SHE MAKES HER OWN CLOTHING, AND
DRESSES IN COLORFUL LINENS AND SILKS."

PROVERBS 31:22 MSG

———

Chapter 13: Classy, Innovative Trendsetter

"She makes for herself coverlets, cushions, and rugs of tapestry. Her clothing is linen, pure and fine, and purple [wool]." (Proverbs 31:22 AMP)

The first thing that came to mind as I read this Scripture was, "She's not waiting on anyone. She makes her own." It occurred to me that so often we are sitting ducks, waiting for an opportunity to knock on our doors, and yet I truly believe God is saying, "I have placed all you need to make it and thrive within you. Stop waiting for someone to invite you to the table, daughter! Open your eyes and see that I have already prepared a table before you in the presence of your enemies!" There is something about purple gowns, fine linen, and silk gowns that says "Royalty, dignitary, money, wealth, favor, beauty, elegance."

This woman is not waiting for someone to tell her she is royalty and a princess warrior! She is not waiting for someone to bestow on her a title that gives her significance and value. Instead, she creates from a place of knowing and understanding that this is who she is! She is the daughter of the King, and thus, she makes for herself that which reflects her known identity, whether others acknowledge it or not. What matters is that SHE KNOWS!!! Not only does she create these as garments for herself, but she also creates things that reflect this for her home. When you walk into her space, you know she is someone to be reckoned with. There is no doubt that she is royalty! When you see her, she oozes the oil of favor and blessings! This is her inheritance, and she is confident in it!

Daughter, oh, that you would see who I see when I look at you and that you would create substance and value from that space of knowing! Understand this, daughter: it is you who will make room for others; it is you who will invite others to the table; it is you who will change the atmosphere with your presence. IT IS YOU! Your validation comes from Me, from who you are, because you come from Me, and no one can take that from you. You only need to believe!

""Her clothing is beautifully knit together - a purple gown of exquisite linen."""" Proverbs 31:22 TPT)

Father, open my sister's eyes to see that she is royalty, that You have clothed her with righteousness and dignity. Address the areas of shame and self-rejection that cause her to dim her light and prevent her from seeing herself as the princess warrior You declared her to be. Let there be a knowing that comes from a profound revelation of her true identity in You. May she look to You for her validation and definition. May she step into rooms with complete confidence in whom You declared her to be, serving from a place of knowing that You delight in her and that she already has Your stamp of approval. Your" ""YES" is all she needs.

Take some time to meditate on the above and allow God to speak to you about your royal lineage! You are a daughter of the King, and He has clothed you with royal robes and bestows on you an identity of great value! What have you been waiting on? From what position have you been creating? Are you still trying to get someone's attention and favor? Or do you recognize that He has already set a table before you, and it is your privilege and honor to decide whom you will invite to your table?

_____
_____
_____
_____
_____
_____
_____
_____
_____
_____
_____
_____
_____

> "She's not waiting on anyone to invite her to the table. She sets her own table and invites others to it."

I AM A NURTURER OF
GIFTS IN ALL THOSE I
ENCOUNTER. I AM
GIFTED WITH THE
SPIRIT OF WISDOM &
INSIGHT TO SEE &
DRAW OUT THE BEST
IN THOSE I SERVE.

CHAPTER 14: NURTURER OF GIFTS

"HER HUSBAND IS GREATLY RESPECTED
WHEN HE DELIBERATES WITH THE CITY
FATHERS."

PROVERBS 31:23 MSG

Chapter 14: Nurturer of gifts

"Her husband is known in the [city's] gates, when he sits among the elders of the land." (Proverbs 31:23 amp)

The women in the life of a man have the ability to make or break them. God has given us as women the ability to draw from men the gift, calling, and anointing in our fathers, brothers, friends, spouses, and sons. We take what they give us and can turn it into trash or gold, regardless of what they bring to us. Even in situations where there is pain and hurt, God has given us the ability to push past the pain to produce life! We should never underestimate the power of influence God has given us as women, particularly in the secret places of conversation and dialogue! Do we encourage, challenge, and build the men in our lives, or do we curse, attack, and destroy them? If he can have a decent conversation with you and hash out his points without fear that you will crush his ideas and thoughts but will instead enhance them and make them better, he will be able to face whomever he has to face in the world out there!

You make him better because God has given you a brilliant mind that sees things he never will without your help! You were created to be his help meet. He needs your skills, your mind, and your presence to accomplish all he was created to do. God knew he could not do it alone...but do you? Do you realize that you have the power to create spaces of influence and respect for the men in your life by how you engage with them and simply by their association with you as a woman of stature and influence? When you understand who and whose you are, you realize that you are not in competition with the men in your life but that a win in your life is a win in theirs and vice versa.

We need each other! With God at our core, we form a formidable force to be reckoned with and can accomplish so much more!

Sister, maybe you have been severely wounded by the men in your life to the point that all you feel you have for them is anger and bitterness and a deep-seated desire to make all men pay for what those select ones did to you. Let me tell you this right now...God understands, and He feels your pain and sorrow. He sees you...all of you! My prayer is that you will see that not all men are evil and have intentions to hurt and abuse and destroy you, but that there are good men out here...not perfect men, not unbroken, but men that genuinely desire to do good, even though they may fail miserably at times.

Daughter, today I want you to know that I have given you the power of life and death, not just over your own life but over the lives of those around you! As you use your voice for good and rise in your gifting and calling, using your hands to build and to uproot that which is not of Me, I will cause goodness to go before you, and you will see the men in your life bloom and become men of valor and respect. Daughter, you are more powerful than you realize!

Father, I pray that my sister finds healing in her relationships with the men in her life and that she discovers and carries with great care the power You have given her to speak into the lives of the men in her life.

Journal what God is speaking to you through this devotional, and share your thoughts on this below. In what ways is God calling you to shift your positioning & influence regarding the men in your life? In what ways is God calling you to shift your positioning & influence regarding the men in your life?

> "When you understand who and whose you are, you realize that you are not in competition with the men in your life but that a win in your life is a win in theirs and vise versa!"

I AM A WEALTH PRODUCER, EQUIPPED WITH ALL I NEED TO GENERATE AN ABUNDANCE OF INCOME THAT BLESSES NOT JUST MY HOUSEHOLD BUT THE WORLD, INCLUDING THOSE WHO SEEK TO HARM ME.

CHAPTER 15: WEALTH PRODUCER

"SHE MAKES AND SELLS LINEN
GARMENTS; SHE DELIVERS BELTS TO
THE MERCHANTS."

PROVERBS 31:24 CSB

Chapter 15: Wealth Producer

"Even her works of righteousness she does for the benefit of her enemies." (Proverbs 31:24 TPT)

Daughter, do you understand that you have the ability to make or break the economy? Yes, you! I have deposited reservoirs of creativity and wealth within you! If you would only take time to sit at my feet and allow me to reveal the ideas and innovations at your fingertips to you!
if you would only stop comparing yourself to others!
You have a unique seed within you that the enemy is after! He knows that what is within you can shift and shape the course of history if you would only wake up to the truth that you carry seed, and your sole responsibility on this earth is to make sure that you bring it to full term and deliver it into this world!

Your dream is not some airy-fairy fantasy; it is the seed of heaven deposited inside you. This is what keeps you awake at night. This is what gives you that sense of discomfort when you are doing something you know is not IT every single time you try to fit someone else's definition and notion of who you are and what you were meant to do. Look only to me!

You were created to be a wealth creator and not just a consumer! You were created to bring life, light, and hope into this world that is consumed with death, darkness, and despair! You were created to shape history and bring heaven to earth with the seed of dreams, ideas, concepts, and gifts unique to you! The world will be better because you exist and dared to act on what I have deposited in you!

Daughter, the world is waiting for you! Your ideas are gold! Even those who hate you and despise you will be blessed and benefit from the seed of your womb! Work it! And watch what I will do through your obedience and diligence! I have every confidence in you! Don't sit on your seed! It is your superpower!

Some dreams may feel like fleeting memories, and some may look dead and buried, but God can breathe life into those things in our lives that are seemingly hopeless, and He is the Resurrection and the Life today! Like Joseph, what the enemy meant for evil and sought to use to destroy you, God is turning around for good for your elevation and promotion to save the lives of many. Invite Him into those dreams and ideas and allow Him to breathe life and hope into them afresh today!

Father, awaken my sister to the truth of who she really is in You! Open her eyes to see the treasure You have deposited within her as seed. Help her to see herself as You see her and help her to recognize the power that she carries in that seed to shift the world with just one seed (decision) at a time. I ask that You awaken faith and hope within her again and breathe life into the dreams, ideas, and concepts You have given her. Please fill her with courage and boldness to step out, be vulnerable with her seed, and trust that what she entrusts to You will bear a harvest in its due season.

Journal your response to the above as a prayer to God about the ideas and innovations that have been dropped into your heart over the years.

In what ways is God leading you to be a wealth produceer and creator rather than just a consumer? What creative ideas and strategies has he given you that have the potential to shift the economic course of not just your life but that of those connected to you?

> "There is a reservoir of creativity and innovation to generate wealth and shift the economy within you."

I AM CLOTHED WITH
STRENGTH & DIGNITY.
GOD HAS BESTOWED
ON ME BOLD POWER &
MAJESTY. JOY IS MY
PORTION & PRAISE IS
MY WEAPON. I FACE
THE FUTURE WITH
CONFIDENCE & GRACE
BECAUSE HE IS WITH
ME.

CHAPTER 16: BOLD & MAJESTIC

"STRENGTH AND DIGNITY ARE HER CLOTHING
AND HER POSITION IS STRONG AND SECURE; AND
SHE SMILES AT THE FUTURE [KNOWING THAT SHE
AND HER FAMILY ARE PREPARED]."

PROVERBS 31:25 AMP

Chapter 16: Bold & Majestic

"Bold power and glorious majesty are wrapped around her as she laughs with joy over latter days." (Proverbs 31:25 TPT)

Just reading that scripture gives me goosebumps! Sis, you are clothed and wrapped in bold power and glorious majesty!!! Let that sink in. Read it again. And again.

I pray that as you read this the love, power, and majesty of God wraps around you and that you feel God's presence so strongly all around you that you know that you are surrounded and that no harm can come near you (Ps. 91). With so much uncertainty surrounding our lives in this season, I pray that you would be filled with joy overflowing as you realize that your future is secure in God's hands! Despite and even amid all that surrounds you, you can have peace and joy because you know that it will be for your good no matter what happens! The MSG says that "she ALWAYS faces tomorrow with a smile." So today, I am praying for peace and that God would silence the voice of anxiety in your spirit and restore joy and the ability to smile at your future because there is a deep reassurance that God has you no matter what!

Daughter, you are beautifully and fearfully made! Daughter, fear does not come from me but is the ploy of the enemy to get you to doubt My heart towards you and cause you to take things into your own hands. Daughter, My Spirit is with you, and you are wrapped in My Presence. No harm shall befall you as you stay under My shadow. Strength and dignity are your portion!

Daughter! You are strong, victorious despite what you see and what others say and despite the voices trying so hard to drown out my voice. Be still, child, and know that I am your God! I am fighting for you! I am on your side! I am for you! Receive my peace today, child, and receive my joy! This is your inheritance in Me! You can smile even as the storm around you rages because you are safe in My arms! I am so fiercely in love with you!

Allow the Word of God to sweep over you today, and allow God to minister peace to your heart! Be still and sit with God for a moment today, and allow yourself to listen to God's voice.

Father, set Your daughter free from every lie of the enemy that has caused her to stay stuck in places of shame, unworthiness, despair, and mourning. Open her eyes to see that Your presence and glory clothe her and that You have prepared her for this moment. Help her weed out the lies and shift her thoughts to Your truths regarding her. May she find joy and laughter and smile in the future, knowing You are with her.

Take some time to sit with the lord and receive from him
that "bold power and majesty" are wrapped around you!
How does receiving that truth into your spirit cause you to
smile at your future?

"
There is a deep
reassurance in knowing that
God has you no matter
what!
"

I AM WISE & KIND,
OVERFLOWING WITH
THE EVIDENCE OF
GOD'S PRESENCE IN
MY LIFE.

CHAPTER 17: WISE & KIND

"SHE OPENS HER MOUTH IN [SKILLFUL AND
GODLY] WISDOM, AND THE TEACHING OF
KINDNESS IS ON HER TONGUE [GIVING COUNSEL
AND INSTRUCTION."

PROVERBS 31:26 AMP

Chapter 17: Wise & Kind

Words are power, and they are life. Words create. Words build or destroy. Words spoken can never be withdrawn. Words communicate the spirit of a person. The Bible mentions the importance of guarding our tongues and monitoring what comes from our mouths and the spirit in which we speak over 129 times in the King James Version. God spoke and the world was created.

"When she speaks she has something worthwhile to say, and she always says it kindly." (Proverbs 31:26 MSG)

You, daughter of the Most High, carry God's DNA within you and have been created in the likeness of the Almighty One, Creator of Heaven and Earth. You are being invited to co-architect and co-create with God, calling things into order and breathing life, healing, peace, and strength into the lives of others. God's resurrection power resides upon your tongue as you submit it to the Holy Spirit. Holy Spirit produces in and through your words of kindness and wisdom that position you as an agent of change in partnership with Abba for the good of those you encounter.

What would happen if you started becoming more aware of what you say and the spirit in which you say these things and realize that with every word, you are planting a seed and reaping a harvest? Would we be more selective in what we put into the atmosphere?

Daughter, My Spirit produces kindness and gentleness within you. When you speak from My presence and follow the example of Jesus, saying only what I tell you to say in each situation, stilling your soul to listen and hear what I am instructing you to say and how I am instructing you to respond,

You will breathe life into every room you step into because wisdom will be in your voice. That is how powerful I have created you to be! You have a choice, daughter, every single time! You can run rampant and do your own thing, OR you can submit your tongue to Me and allow Me to work in and through you to shift atmospheres and bring about change. But it starts with you, child! It begins with your willingness to sit with Me, drink from Me, and pour from your place of overflow and saturation from My presence. Everything you desire is within your reach - healing, wholeness, peace, joy, love, and restoration! It is in your tongue! What will you use your words for today?

Father, may my sister recognize the power You have placed in her mouth to shift atmospheres and speak into being Your purposes. May she submit to Your purification of her tongue that she may only speak what You tell her to speak that pertains to life. May she not be moved to speak from her emotions sowing seed unto death, but may every word she speaks be strategically aligned with Your Word. May she lean into Your Spirit of Wisdom and Revelation to speak to those things that cannot be seen in the physical realm but to bring heaven to earth in the lives of those You have assigned to her with the words she prophetically speaks over them. May she not be moved by what she sees, but may everything she does flow from what she hears You say.

Take some time today to sit with God and evaluate how you have used your tongue and words, and the spirit with which you have spoken. Ask God to help you use the power given to you to breathe life into your world and those around you. Journal these conversations, be still, and listen to God's voice speaking to you in this moment.

> Your words are seeds that have the power to birth life or death. There is creative power in your tongue to shift atmospheres and call into order chaos. Choose your seed wisely.

I AM WATCHFUL AND
ATTENTIVE. MY HANDS
ARE ENGAGED FULLY
IN MY ASSIGNMENT. I
ATTEND TO MY
BUSINESS & DO NOT
ENGAGE IN IDLENESS.

CHAPTER 18: WATCHFUL, ATTENTIVE & FOCUSED

"SHE WATCHES OVER THE WAYS OF HER HOUSEHOLD AND MEETS EVERY NEED THEY HAVE."

PROVERBS 31:27 TPT

Chapter 18: Watchful, Attentive & Focused

"She keeps an eye on everyone in her household, and keeps them all busy and productive." (Proverbs 31:27 MSG)

It starts at home! Yes, sis...handle your business at home first. And then comes the rest! Now, I will be the first to admit that I do not get this right more than 60% of the time...because somewhere, someone told us that being busy and not having time for the things that matter most was cool! It is totally NOT COOL! Yesterday, I learned that a family that I admire for their work in empowering and equipping people to walk in purpose filed for divorce in May after over 18 years of marriage, and to be honest, sis, my heart broke! I had a conversation with God last night saying, "Lord, please do not let me expend so much energy in building something that causes me to lose what matters most."

For single or unmarried people, you may be asking what that has to do with you. Your family is not just a husband or children, but it is those that are in your inner circle that God has connected you to for His purposes...those relationships that He has gifted you with that feed and nourish your soul that you push to the back burner when life pulls on you!

Daughter, there are those that I have assigned to you specifically – whose purpose is attached to yours. Attend to them and start with those first! Many times, you run yourself ragged, serving the purposes of others that drain you and are not connected to My purpose for your life, to the end that you have nothing to pour into those I have assigned to you. Be occupied with the things that are on My heart. Be active in things that are connected to your purpose and destiny.

People are counting on you to step up and show up in your destiny. Stop and take inventory, child, and allow me to guide you to the right relationships and to give you perspective on the purpose I intended for that connection.

Father, help my sister awaken to the truth that You have created and chosen her for this moment. Help her recognize that she is not a mistake and that her positioning is not a mistake. Please help her to take authority over the territory that You have assigned to her. Lord, deal with the areas of resistance and resentment that cause her to get stuck in places of comparison, discontent, and self-pity. Help her realize that You believe in her and invite her to partner with You to bring people out of places of darkness into the light. Help her recognize the value of the gift in her and to exercise it with wisdom in the areas You have assigned her to.

In what ways have you got caught in places of idleness (gossip, discontent, self-pity), minimizing the value of what you have been given? How have you left your post vacant because you felt what you had to bring to the table was not worth the time and effort?

> Daughter, there are those that I have assigned to you specifically – whose purpose is attached to yours. Attend to them and start with those first!

I AM RESPECTED & PRAISEWORTHY. MY LIFE IS AN AUTHENTIC EXPRESSION OF THE GRACE OF GOD & I WALK WITH HUMILITY & MERCY IN MY DAILY INTERACTIONS WITH THOSE I LOVE & SERVE.

CHAPTER 19: RESPECTED & PRAISEWORTHY

"HER CHILDREN RESPECT AND BLESS HER; HER
HUSBAND JOINS IN WITH WORDS OF PRAISE"

PROVERBS 31:28 MSG

Chapter 19: Respected & Praiseworthy

"Her sons and daughters arise in one accord to extol her virtues, and her husband arises to speak of her in glowing terms." (Proverbs 31:28 TPT)

As one who used to work with children every day, almost all day... I can tell you this - you cannot fake it with the kids! You can pretend with everyone in your world, but your kids know the real deal, and they will keep it real with you 100% of the time! Then your hubby or partner...well... let's say, "No one knows the real you like your family!" The you with no makeup, the you when you are happy and sad and angry, the you with plenty and with little, the you in all four seasons...they have seen it all. And if all they have to say about you after all of that is good, and they can mention your virtues...then sis, you are it!

So, I will be transparent and let you know that if you talk to my family, they will probably tell you the good, the bad, and the ugly...but I know without a shadow of a doubt that they know now that I love them with all my heart and would do absolutely anything for them. The truth is this has not always been the case...there were many years when I was self-righteous, selfish, and self-centered. And years, when I brought my family so much grief and pain but refused to see it because I was stuck in my justification mode - I felt I had a right to act how I was acting, and boy, was it messed up!!! Yes, sis...Christians like you and me can be mean and ugly and still profess that we love Jesus! Ummmm... Thank you, Lord, for grace and mercy!

Something about falling flat on your face wakes you up to the truth about love and humility! Some of us are so stuck up high on our self-righteous horses that we are of no use to God because we are totally faking it, and there is no truth in us. Sometimes, it takes a hard fall for us to wake up and see the log in our own eyes enough to deal with ourselves instead of being so preoccupied with the sins of others.

So, instead of being judgmental and critical about how others are living their lives, how about we allow God to search our hearts and bring us face to face with the reality of our own sin and allow God's love to change us and make us more like Jesus? Maybe when we start actually loving and serving like Jesus, the world will begin to see God's goodness in us and start praising God because of our lives.

Father, I pray that You would shine the light on my sister and clear the mirror for her so that she can see the areas in her life that You are inviting her to bring into submission to You – especially her emotions and triggers. I ask that You open her heart to receiving Your grace and kindness that empowers her to do what You have done for her and that others will be blessed by her willingness to be humble, broken, and vulnerable. Heal the areas in her soul that cause her to build up walls of defensiveness and self-protection, and let Your love soften the hard and dry places so that she can receive from You all that she needs to truly bless the people in her immediate world first and then the rest of the world.

What is your story, sis? What would those closest to you say about you when they talk about you? What would your family say? What are some areas that you need to invite God into and allow Him to heal and soften your heart and soul? Journal what God is speaking to you today, and if you feel like you can, please share some of your thoughts below. I love you, and I am praying for you.

_____
_____
_____
_____
_____
_____
_____
_____
_____
_____
_____
_____

" What would happen if you allow people to really get to know you? What would those who know you best have to say about you? "

I AM UNIQUE &
DIFFERENT. I EMBRACE
MY IDENTITY AS ONE
THAT STANDS APART
FROM THE CROWD. I
AM ONE OF A KIND,
DEMONSTRATING
INTEGRITY &
EXCELLENCE IN ALL I
SAY & DO.

CHAPTER 20: IN A CLASS OF HER OWN

"MANY WOMEN HAVE DONE WONDERFUL
THINGS, BUT YOU'VE OUTCLASSED THEM
ALL!"

PROVERBS 31:29 MSG

Chapter 20: In a Class of Her Own

"There are many valiant and noble ones, but you have ascended above them all." (Proverbs 31:29 TPT)

Standing out is uncomfortable and can often feel incredibly lonely. Being called upon by our Father to walk the path of destiny and purpose is a call to walk the untrodden, unfamiliar path and often comes with the high price of not fitting in and blending in with the crowd. You will be misunderstood, judged, and like a performer on a stage with the spotlight shining on them, every mistake and flaw will be highlighted, reviewed, discussed, and put on blast, which can be humiliating and shame-inducing. And yet, this is where He is calling you to, daughter!

You are being called to step out of the shadows and into the light so that others can see the brilliance He has placed within you. I know you are comfortable in the background, pushing others forward into their purpose and destiny, but now is the time for you to come out and shine even more brilliantly. The only way to do this without fear is to remain hidden in Him and submitted to Him. This may mean speaking up when the pressure to keep silent is fierce, bringing things into the light that others would prefer remain hidden, experiencing rejection when you present ideas that are outside of the box and unfamiliar, and experiencing abandonment when the challenge feels unrelenting and daunting.

Here's the promise and reassurance: Daughter, when you walk with Me, you will do exploits and conquer territories that no one else would even dare to venture into. Daughter, My hand upon your life, and the wisdom, insight, and revelation I will impart to you will set you above your peers. The road may be lonely, but know this: I AM WITH YOU ALWAYS! You will never be alone! My glory and presence will go before you, cover you, and set you apart! What is for you is secure. I will do wonderful things through you, and there will be no doubt it is My doing. This is your inheritance in Me!

Father, I pray for my sister today as she steps boldly and fiercely into all You created her to be, that she would hide completely in You. That Your glory would be her covering and that Your presence would go with her into every arena You send her into. I pray that she would experience Your favor that sets her apart and above her peers in supernatural and exceptional ways and that there can be no doubt she walks with You. I pray that she would be fearless in what You tell her to do, though they may never have been done before. May she rely entirely on You for wisdom, trusting in Your infinite power to bring into completion and fruition all that You impart in vision for her to do. May she run her race with diligence and complete her assignment with grace so that generations to come may experience the blessings and inheritance You desire to pass on them. May she continuously know Your presence and approval as she remains submitted and surrendered to You.

In what ways are you feeling the nudging of the Father, calling you out of the shadows into the light? In what ways is He challenging you to come up higher and venture into new territories with Him to do what has never been done before? Will you dare to trust Him and go?

> "
> Daughter, when you walk with me you will do exploits and conquer territories that no one else would even dare to venture into.
> "

I AM SUBMITTED IN
REVERENCE TO HOLY
SPIRIT & WALK
CONTINUALLY IN THE
FEAR OF GOD.
I AM BEAUTIFUL FROM
THE INSIDE OUT.

CHAPTER 21: SUBMITTED IN REVERENCE

"CHARM IS DECEPTIVE AND BEAUTY IS FLEETING,
BUT A WOMAN WHO FEARS THE LORD WILL BE
PRAISED. GIVE HER THE REWARD OF HER LABOR,
AND LET HER WORKS PRAISE HER AT THE CITY
GATES."

PROVERBS 31:30-31 CSB

Chapter 21: Submitted in Reverence

As we wrap up this journey together, what if we were to see ourselves through the eyes of the One that created us and realize that what we are searching for has already been created as part of our intricate design by the All-knowing God of Heaven and Earth? All we have to do is walk in the fullness of who God says we are and occupy the positions that have been set aside for us by our Maker from the beginning of time! Our only responsibility is to walk with the Lord and to live in awe, wonder, fear, and reverence for the Spirit of God! To see God in everything and in ALL! God holds the world together by the Word... the DNA of heaven holds together every cell, ligament, fiber of your being!

"Charm can be misleading, and beauty is vain and so quickly fades, but this virtuous woman lives in the wonder, awe, and fear of the Lord. She will be praised throughout eternity." (Proverbs 31:30 TPT)

I absolutely loved reading this passage in all the different versions because something awakened in me as I read in bold letters, "GOD SEES ME!!!" Yes, sis!

God is in every single space of air and substance...God fills everything! There is not one space of existence outside of the Spirit of God! You and I are living and breathing in the realm of God's being! Take a moment and let that sink in! When we live each moment of our lives in awe of God, in awareness of God, in full cognizance of God in every moment and space, our whole world shifts, and we realize we do not need to strive to thrive; we simply need to be! Be who you were created to be, sis! Breathe God in and breathe God out! In every season of life, God is! And because God is you are! All that you touch is blessed and shall prosper!

Daughter, I see all that you are and all that you are doing! Nothing misses me! Nothing is hidden from me! I see you! Everything about you! You are radiant daughter, and you are glorious in beauty and elegance! There are so many beautiful women in this world that sometimes you feel that I don't see you, that I missed you, that I overlooked you....but believe me when I tell you that I know you by name! I know every hair on your head! I know every cell in your body! I know every desire, every longing, every dream, every hope, EVERYTHING! And I desire that you receive the credit that is due to you! Do not give up, child, when you feel your hard work goes unnoticed! Just keep on doing good and wait and see what I am about to do for you! You have my ear, and you have my heart! Nothing and no one will dare to stand in the way of my favor on your life as you remain connected and submitted to me! I have your back! You will live to see my goodness in your life! This is my promise! Rest in it!

Father, open my sister's eyes further into seeing herself as You see her in the days ahead. Let her operate from a place of rest and trust in Your finished work, and cease all forms of striving and stress. Let her know that You are within her and that as long as she abides in You, You will make her way prosperous! It is done! It is finished! And the end has already been declared as one of victory!

Take some time today to sit with God and go back over your journey over the last 21 days! What has God been teaching you about yourself through this devotional?

> Daughter, I see all that you are
> and all that you are doing!
> Nothing misses me! Nothing is
> hidden from me! I see you!!!

Dear Beautiful & Unleashed One,

THANK YOU FOR TAKING THE TIME TO GO
THROUGH THIS DEVOTIONAL. I PRAY THAT
YOU WERE ENCOURAGED AND
EMPOWERED TO SEE YOURSELF FROM A
DIFFERENT PERSPECTIVE. I PRAY THAT
THIS SHIFT IN PERSPECTIVE HAS
EMPOWERED YOU TO LIVE YOUR LIFE OUT
IN A DIFFERENT MANNER - ONE THAT
FLOWS FROM A PLACE OF ALREADY
HAVING ALL YOU NEED TO FULFILL YOUR
GOD-GIVEN ASSIGNMENT RATHER THAN
STRIVING TO PROVE OR ACHIEVE
SOMETHING YOU FEEL IS LACKING IN YOU.
MAY GOD CONTINUE TO HEAL AND
RESTORE BROKEN AREAS IN YOUR LIFE,
SETTING YOU FREE TO BE ALL YOU WERE
CREATED TO BE FROM THE BEGINNING OF
TIME!

I WOULD LOVE TO HEAR FROM YOU.
PLEASE FEEL FREE TO EMAIL ME AND LET ME
KNOW HOW THIS DEVOTIONAL HAS
IMPACTED YOUR LIFE AT
CONNECT@DESTINY-CONNECTIONS.COM.

·

Made in the USA
Columbia, SC
25 October 2024

44671473R00061